Eye Remember:
A Baby-Boomer's Scrapbook

By JoAnn Semones

DEDICATION

For Julie, who remembers, too

Eye Remember: A Baby-Boomer's Scrapbook
© 2008 JoAnn Semones. All Rights Reserved.

All illustrations are copyright of their respective owners, and are also reproduced here in the spirit of publicity. Whilst we have made every effort to acknowledge specific credits whenever possible, we apologize for any omissions, and will undertake every effort to make any appropriate changes in future editions of this book if necessary.

No part of this book may be reproduced in any form or by any means, electronic, mechanical, digital, photocopying or recording, except for the inclusion in a review, without permission in writing from the publisher.

Published by
BearManor Media
P O Box 71426
Albany, GA 31708

ISBN 1-59393-250-2

Printed in the United States of America.

Book & cover design by Darlene & Dan Swanson of Van-garde Imagery, Inc.

Contents:

INTRODUCTION	7
AMERICAN HEROES	9
Not Expendable - John Wayne 9	
Baseball's Diamond - Joe DiMaggio 10	
Bravest of The Brave - Audie Murphy 14	
Legendary Soldier - General Douglas MacArthur 16	
MUSIC! MUSIC! MUSIC!	19
Lady of Spain – Dick Contino 19	
Love Me Tender – Elvis Presley 21	
Chances Are – Johnny Mathis 23	
Downtown - Petula Clark 25	
Sweet Linda Divine – Linda Tillery 27	
TELEVISION ICONS	29
Gunsmoke – Dennis Weaver 29	
Wyatt Earp – Hugh O'Brien 31	
Tales Of Wells Fargo – Dale Robertson 33	
Man From UNCLE – Robert Vaughn 35	
The FBI – Efrem Zimbalist, Jr. & William Reynolds 37	
Adam 12 – Martin Milner & Kent McCord 39	

AWAKENINGS 43
    Beacon of Light – Countess Alexandra Tolstoy   43
    Spiritual Quest - Reverend Troy Perry   45
    Raising Consciousness - Ms. Gloria Steinem   47
    Building Character And Communities – Prince Philip   49

THE KENNEDYS 51
    Making A Difference - Robert F. Kennedy   51
    Working Together - Ethel Kennedy   53
    The Last Brother - Edward M. Kennedy   55
    Sister Extraordinaire - Patricia Kennedy Lawford   56
    Kennedy Legacy - Theodore C. Sorensen   58

CALIFORNIA LEADERS 61
    Citizen-Politician – Ronald Reagan   61
    Big Daddy – Jesse Unruh   63
    Mr. San Francisco – Joseph Alioto   65
    No Lightweight – John Tunney   67
    His Father's Son - Barry Goldwater, Jr.   68

PRESIDENTIAL HOPEFULS 71
    Frontrunner – Edmund Muskie   71
    Powerhouse – Wilbur Mills   73
    Great Orator – John Connally   75
    Well-Mannered Mayor – John Lindsay   76

ABOUT THE AUTHOR 79
PHOTO CREDITS 81
BIBLIOGRAPHY 85

INTRODUCTION

The eye of the camera lens is a window to our world. Through it, we see beauty, tragedy, and the passing of our lives.

Sometimes, if we are especially fortunate, we are privileged to view fleeting moments in history. I have experienced a few of those moments. *Eye Remember* is a personal glimpse at the people, places, and events that shaped my generation, a generation of post World War II "baby-boomers."

Born on an Army Air Force base in the mid-1940s, I traveled from post to post with my parents and younger sister. When we returned from Japan, where my father was part of the Occupation Forces, we settled in California. There, I grew up with the first generation inseparable from a television set. I watched everything from Beany and Cecil to Elvis.

In the 1960s, I was an idealistic college student and political activist. My school years were punctuated with the assassinations of John F. Kennedy, Martin Luther King, Jr., and Robert F. Kennedy, the war in Viet Nam, civil disobedience, and the race to the moon.

After graduation, I worked as small town newspaper reporter and photographer.

Later, I enjoyed a stint on Capitol Hill as press secretary to a California Congressman who was my local Representative and a ranking member of the House Ways and Means and Small Business Committees.

Through it all, my camera was a constant companion. This volume contains photos, all from my personal collection, and profiles of celebrities, activists, and political leaders from those times. They colored my life and the lives of many others.

AMERICAN HEROES

When World War II threw the United States into sudden global conflict, the country needed heroes. On the home front and on the battle field, they appeared. The deeds of these heroes were interwoven with the lives and sacrifices of many American families.

John Wayne embodied American fighting spirit and patriotism. Joe DiMaggio gave the nation hope. Audie Murphy was the youthful boy next door whose gallantry became the stuff of legends. In settling the aftermath of war, a new era began when General Douglas MacArthur rebuilt an empire that was once a bitter enemy.

Not Expendable - John Wayne

My father, along with countless others, formed the bombing crews of the legendary "Flying Fortress." During World War II, thousands of courageous young men swarmed the skies of Europe in B-17s. Many failed to make the round trip home. Some, like my father, continued to climb back into the heavens, brace themselves against grim odds, and complete 50 missions.

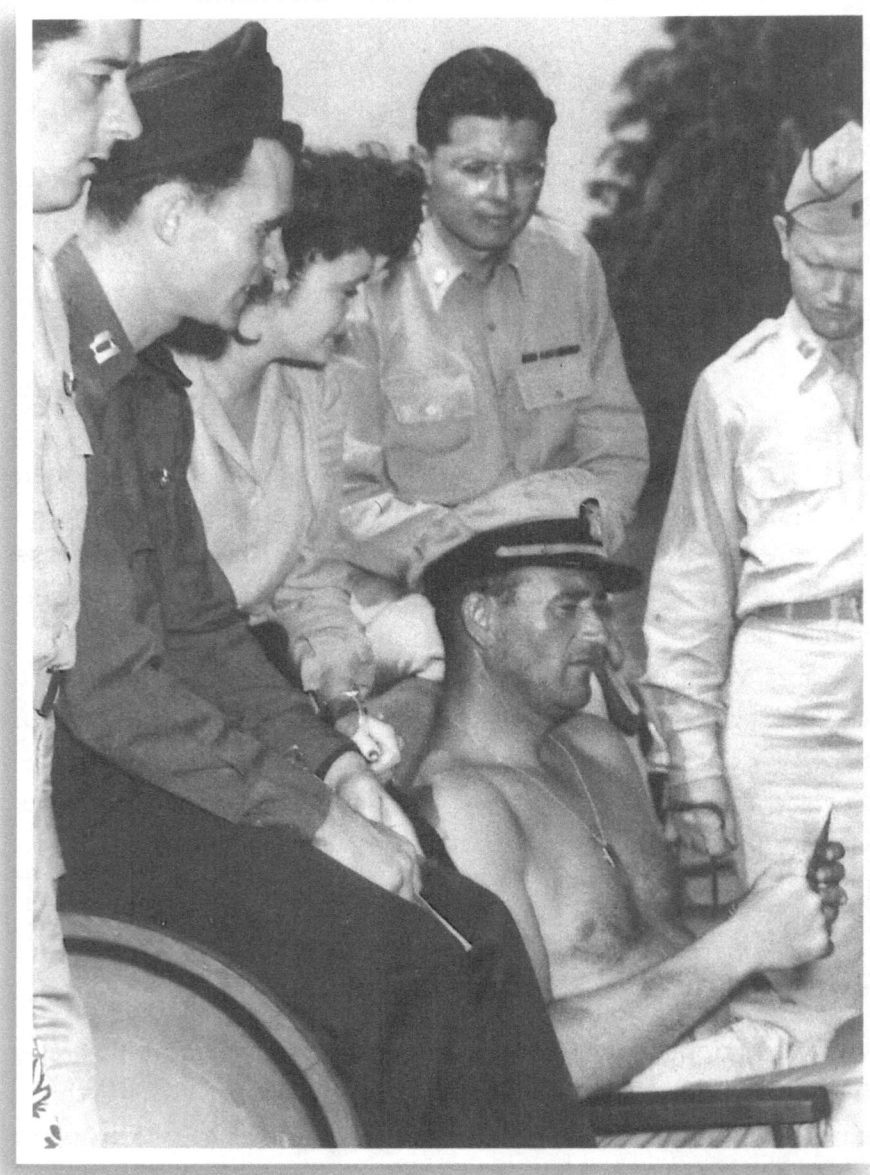

John Wayne's battle scenes inspired a nation at war. During a break in filming "They Were Expendable" in Miami Beach, Florida in 1944, Wayne chats with servicemen. George and Grace Semones, the author's parents, are sitting to the left.

After graduating from the Army Air Corps's bombardier school, he joined a flight crew training for overseas duty. In March of 1944, with a combat assignment imminent, he married his sweetheart in the Post Chapel at Langley Field, Virginia. The newlyweds encountered actor John Wayne filming the naval war epic, "They Were Expendable," while honeymooning in Miami Beach, Florida.

On meeting Wayne, my father quipped, "I hope fervently that I'm not expendable." Wayne drawled, "None of you guys are." Neither was he.

Later that year, Wayne spent three months touring forward positions in the Pacific theater of war. He wanted to become an officer in the Navy not just portray one, but an old football injury prevented it. While the Navy may have lost a fine officer, America gained inspirational battle films. To those at home and others around the world, John Wayne was more than a magnetic screen personality. He was the symbol of the determined American fighting man.

Years after the war, when Emperor Hirohito of Japan visited the United States, he sought out John Wayne, paying tribute to the man who represented our country's success in combat. When Wayne died in 1979 a Tokyo newspaper ran the headline, "Mr. America Passes On."

Baseball's Diamond - Joe DiMaggio

Seeing Joe DiMaggio in his later years still held the same magic as watching him in his prime. No one could ever forget how he heartened the nation's spirits at a time when it was needed most. In doing so, he became a hero in his own right.

DiMaggio's early beginnings mirrored that of many families

who formed the nation's core during the Depression years. Dropping out of school, he fled the family fishing business to play baseball at the dairy wagon parking lot near San Francisco's Fisherman's Wharf. "We used rocks for bases," DiMaggio recalled. "It was quite a scramble among 20 of us kids to scrape up a nickel to buy a roll of bicycle tape to patch up the ball each day."

After joining the New York Yankees in 1936, the sensational rookie became the only athlete in North American professional sports to be on four World Championship teams in his first four full seasons. In 1941, as America readied itself for war, DiMaggio embarked on one of the greatest feats in national sports. Nicknamed the "Yankee Clipper" for his graceful play on the field, his 56 game hitting streak captivated the country.

In 1942, he enlisted in the Army. Although DiMaggio asked for no special treatment, the Army thought him more valuable at home than overseas. Assigned to Special Services, he continued to play baseball and boosted troop morale with his inspired athletic performances. If Joe kept winning, Americans felt they could, too.

After World War II, DiMaggio toured Japan as a goodwill ambassador with fellow San Franciscan "Lefty" O'Doul and other professional baseball players. General Douglas MacArthur, the Supreme Commander of the Allied Powers in Japan, asked them to be the "link in the chain" across the Pacific to help heal the wounds of war.

"Joe DiMaggio, the son of Italian immigrants, gave every American something to believe in. He became the very symbol of American grace, power, and skill," baseball commissioner Bud Selig observed when DiMaggio died in 1999. "I have no doubt that when future generations look back at the best of America in the 20th Century, they will think of the Yankee Clipper and all he achieved."

Joe DiMaggio became the symbol of a nation's hope. After a sensational career in baseball, he often played golf at the coastal links of Half Moon Bay, California. In October 1994, he led the city's renowned Pumpkin Festival Parade as Grand Marshall.

Bravest of The Brave - Audie Murphy

The somber roll of muffled drums trailing a black draped caisson still echoes in my mind. On a radiant morning following Memorial Day 1971, the most decorated soldier of World War II is being laid to rest. Gunfire sounds in salute as the flag draped casket, wreathed in red, white and blue carnations, is placed beneath a giant oak tree in Arlington National Cemetery. When the last volley is fired and the flag folded and presented, the military band disappears slowly over the hill to strains of "America the Beautiful."

Audie Murphy was the bravest of the brave, a larger-than-life hero. Shy and unassuming, baby-faced and slight of build, in combat he was as scrappy as they come. As part of the Army's 3rd Infantry Division, he served in the North African, European, and Mediterranean Campaigns of World War II. Murphy won more medals for valor, including the Medal of Honor, than any other serviceman.

Born the sixth of twelve children to a sharecropper in Kingston, Texas, Murphy faced a hard-scrabble existence. As a youth, he dropped out of school, working on the farm and doing odd jobs. He also became a crack shot with a rifle, hunting rabbits and squirrels to help put food on the family table. After being rejected by the Marines and the paratroopers for being too small, he enlisted in the Army and insisted on being a combat soldier.

Under conditions of extreme mental and physical stress, confronted with obstacles nearly impossible to overcome, he gave nothing less than his best. In the process, he gave the rest of the world lessons in courage. Murphy epitomized the gallantry of U.S. fighting forces: "Ordinary people performing conspicuous and extraordinary acts reflecting great credit upon themselves and their country."

American Heroes 15

Audie Murphy was the most decorated soldier of World War II. Always humble about his combat feats, the Medal of Honor winner received a hero's funeral at Arlington National Cemetery in 1971.

His fearlessness earned him 33 awards and decorations, including three Purple Hearts. Characteristically, Murphy was humble about his achievements. "The real heroes," he declared, "are the ones with wooden crosses."

Legendary Soldier - General Douglas MacArthur

In May of 1949, my father was assigned to the U.S. Occupation forces in Japan. Shortly after arriving, he captured the imposing presence of General Douglas MacArthur outside the Allied Command Headquarters in downtown Tokyo. Strategically located across the moat surrounding the Emperor's Palace, the new square pillared building was formerly the home of the Dai Ichi Insurance Company.

"I went into Tokyo this afternoon. I took the camera and waited in front of General MacArthur's Headquarters where he and his staff draw up their edicts," my father wrote. "Waiting to see 'Doug' is a routine event. People line up, watch him make his grand exit and take pictures. I think I got a good shot of him."

Never has a soldier's life so completely reflected a nation's military history. A graduate of West Point, MacArthur lived his entire life in the Army and served eight Presidents. He was the most decorated American officer of World War I, presided over the Japanese surrender which ended World War II, and was the principal architect in rebuilding a devastated empire.

After World War II, MacArthur was appointed Supreme Commander of the Allied Powers in Japan. His position was, and still is, unprecedented. No other professional soldier has been allowed to exercise civil responsibility and absolute control over almost

General Douglas MacArthur lifted Japan from the ashes of war. The brilliant military strategist led Occupation forces in rebuilding the same empire he helped to defeat. He is shown making his "grand exit" from Allied Command Headquarters in Tokyo.

80 million people. Under his leadership, Japan instituted a democratic government and charted an economic course that has made it an international industrial power.

"It is my earnest hope, and indeed the hope of all mankind, that a better world shall emerge out of the bloodshed and carnage of the past," MacArthur said, "a world founded upon faith and understanding, a world dedicated to the dignity of man and the fulfillment of his most cherished wish – for freedom, tolerance, and justice."

MacArthur died in Washington, D.C. in 1964. He was 84.

MUSIC! MUSIC! MUSIC!

The 1950s and 1960s revolutionized American popular music. From raucous to romantic, a host of new sounds emerged. This is a sampling of the era's diverse performers.

Dick Contino made accordion playing incredibly sexy. Elvis Presley's raw energy changed the musical world forever. Johnny Mathis epitomized class and romance. Petula Clark's fans followed her "Downtown." Linda Tillery's psychedelic/soul band took fans on a different kind of trip.

Lady of Spain – Dick Contino

For a brief moment in the early 1950s, Dick Contino was a star. Brawny and handsome enough to have his own groupies, he made playing the accordion unbelievably sexy. Hollywood columnist Erskine Johnson observed, "He looks down at his accordion the way Gilbert used to look down at Garbo."

Born in Fresno, California, Contino began his music career in the late 1940s performing in Los Angeles talent shows. He soon earned a reputation as the "world's greatest accordion player."

Dick Contino was King of the Accordian. His good looks and gyrations on stage made him an unlikely sex symbol. Still vigorous, he plays at festivals like this one at San Francisco's Fisherman's Wharf.

Contino's big break came when he gyrated around the stage and his fingers flew through the air playing "Lady of Spain."

He became so popular that he appeared on television's well-known Sunday night variety program, "The Ed Sullivan Show," a record 48 times. "I'm very ambitious," Contino admitted. "I want to do everything I can with my music and find new ways and mediums for it."

Contino's success was interrupted when he was drafted during the Korean War. After ignoring the draft notice, he was jailed for draft dodging. Ultimately, he served in the Armed Forces, but the scandal dealt his career a serious blow. Contino lost his recording contracts and his promising film career dropped to the realm of B-movies. He described one of his films as "a class Z picture."

A proficient virtuoso and a skilled jazz improviser, Contino continues to perform regularly throughout the United States. His repertoire includes a still lusty rendition of "Lady of Spain" as well as Italian songs. One fan squealed, "He's sort of a Stallone-Elvis cross."

Love Me Tender – Elvis Presley

Elvis Presley was, and still is, the King of Rock and Roll. His plaintive delivery, flamboyant moves, and innovative coupling of rhythm and blues melodies transformed American music.

When Elvis first swiveled onto center stage, many viewed him as a moral menace.

After all, the 1950s were a time when hair was short, suits were made of gray flannel, and public sexual displays were rare. "He's a 21 year old hillbilly who howls, mumbles, coos and cries," Life magazine snorted. "He uses the bump and grind routine usually seen only in burlesque."

Three times Elvis made headlines on television's popular variety program, "The Ed Sullivan Show." In September 1956, his wild hip gyrations and raw energy sent shock waves through the viewing public, attracting a record 60 million viewers. Presley came back twice in 1957, but his final appearance was censored as too suggestive. As a result, he was filmed only above the waist.

"Music should be something that makes you gotta move, inside or outside," Elvis shrugged. "Rock and roll music, you can't help but move to it. That's what happens to me. I can't help it."

Presley was also destined for a career on the silver screen. In April of 1956, his chance arrived when Hollywood producer Hal Wallis gave him a screen test. When Elvis was asked to read a part

Elvis Presley was King of Rock and Roll. His flamboyant moves and unique musical interpretations transformed American music forever. This photo was handed out in theaters for Elvis' 1956 film debut in "Love Me Tender." My sister and I wore pony-tails in honor of the occasion.

from "The Rainmaker," he told Wallis he didn't like the character and wanted to play one more like himself. A few months later, they signed a deal for "Love Me Tender," a film in which Elvis played a passionate, naive young man destined to die young.

When Elvis died at only 42 on August 28, 1977, he left behind not only a legion of fans who love him, but a musical legacy few have surpassed. "Elvis is the greatest cultural force in the 20th Century," composer Leonard Bernstein declared. "He introduced the beat to everything, music, language, clothes. It was a whole new social revolution. The '60s came from it."

Chances Are – Johnny Mathis

Suave and understated, Johnny Mathis was as romantic a crooner as they come. Some fans swooned and called him "Johnny Mmm."

Mathis was discovered by George Avakian while singing part-time in a San Francisco nightclub. Without hesitating, Avakian sent a now famous telegram to Columbia Records saying, "Have found phenomenal 19 year-old boy who could go all the way. Send blank contracts."

There was just one problem. Mathis, a track and field star at San Francisco State College, had been invited to compete for qualification in Australia's upcoming 1956 Olympics. "I asked my parents what I should do," he recalled. "They told me I was on the right track and singing is what I should do."

From the beginning, Mathis had definite ideas about his singing and his approach to showmanship. He was a particularly composed performer on stage, quite a change from the more dynamic pop singers of the day. "I was always adamant about the fact that

Johnny Mathis' songs expressed the essence of romance. His recordings of ballads like "Chances Are" made him the first black entertainer to become a millionaire before age 21. He appears here at a concert at San Francisco's Davies Hall.

I was not an entertainer," Mathis explained. "I was a singer. Nothing would get in the way of the music."

He became a star in 1955 when "Chances Are," his third single record, was a hit. Mathis soon earned the distinction of being the first black entertainer to become a millionaire before the age of

21. In 1958, he also became the first recording artist to have a "greatest hits" album released. The album peaked at number one on Billboard's pop album charts and stayed in the charts for nearly ten years, a feat unequaled until 1973.

Johnny Mathis still tours widely and his soft, romantic approach continues to appeal to a wide spectrum of music fans. As Frank Sinatra noted, "His voice is one of the most distinctive and instantly recognizable in the world. He epitomizes class and romance."

Downtown - Petula Clark

With "a voice as sweet as a chapel bell," Petula Clark first broke into the limelight during World War II. She was six when she began entertaining troops in England.

By the time she turned nine, Clark had performed in more than 200 shows all over the country. "I was sort of a mascot of the GIs based in London, but I was singing for everyone," she mused. "We traveled in troop trains and slept in the luggage racks."

In the 1950s, Clark made her film debut, became a star of English radio and television, and cut her first record, a version of Teresa Brewer's "Music! Music! Music!" In 1965, her recording of "Downtown" reached Number One in the United States, and catapulted her into international stardom. "Downtown" was the first of 15 consecutive Top 40 hits she scored in America. "It was great," she acknowledged, "and at the same time, it complicated my life."

Clark stayed on the international pop charts longer than any other artist – 51 years.

She continues to keep a full schedule of television and night-

Petula Clark took her fans "Downtown," then stayed on the international pop charts for over 50 years. She also appeared in several stage productions, including "Sunset Boulevard." She was snapped during the opening night reception in San Francisco.

club dates, and has appeared in numerous films and stage productions.

For all of her achievements in the post-"Downtown" era, Clark understands the importance of that one song and just how much it has come to define her career. "It was extraordinary," she commented. "People just happened to fall in love with this song, and I guess with me along with it."

Sweet Linda Divine – Linda Tillery

San Francisco native Linda Tillery launched her professional singing career in 1967 when, still a teenager, she became lead singer for The Loading Zone.

"Linda Tillery's vocals are a cross between Janis Joplin and any number of jazzy mid-'60s crooners," one fan observed. "The group is often linked with psychedelic bands, but they tend to go for blues and jazz numbers. The songs are very strong."

A gender-integrated psychedelic/soul band, The Loading Zone was something of a departure from Tillery's musical roots. Her

Linda Tillery's sweet voice was divine. A versatile performer and musical pioneer, she was lead singer for a psychedelic/soul band before turning to women's music and to traditional Afro-American music. She is shown with the author at a party in San Francisco.

early musical education was anchored in traditional sounds of artists such as Muddy Waters and Dinah Washington.

Modeled after Sly and the Family Stone, The Loading Zone often opened for headliners such as Janis Joplin, Big Brother and the Holding Company, and The Grateful Dead. After two albums and nationwide tours with the band, Tillery released her solo debut album, "Sweet Linda Divine," on CBS Records in 1970 to enthusiastic reviews and high praise.

In the early 1980s, Tillery pioneered the "women's music movement" serving as a staff producer at Olivia Records, and performing on dozens of records. Creating her own group, Linda Tillery and Her Band, she also continued singing with such artists as Kenny Loggins, Boz Scaggs, and Linda Ronstadt, and collaborating with Santana and Joan Baez.

Today, Tillery is a prominent figure in women's music and sings with her five-woman a cappella ensemble, Cultural Heritage Choir. The ensemble presents a highly spirited and innovative journey through the riches of traditional Afro-American music. "The music and I were waiting to be reconnected," Tillery reflected. "We were waiting to find each other again."

TELEVISION ICONS

During the 1950s and 1960s, several television series claimed a position of prominence in popular culture. "Gunsmoke," "The Life and Legend of Wyatt Earp," and "Tales of Wells Fargo" were billed as adult westerns. "The Man From UNCLE" was an innovative spy thriller. "The FBI" and "Adam 12" highlighted the everyday heroics of law enforcement officers. Each attracted cult audiences for decades to come.

The men who starred in these roles, Dennis Weaver, Hugh O'Brien, Dale Robertson, Robert Vaughn, Efrem Zimbalist, Jr., William Reynolds, Martin Milner, and Kent McCord, were not only television icons, but war veterans, civic leaders, and political activists.

Gunsmoke – Dennis Weaver

Affecting a limp and drawling, "Mis-ter Dil-lon," Dennis Weaver created one of television's most memorable characters. As Deputy Marshal Chester Goode in the classic western series "Gunsmoke," the lanky actor became everyone's favorite side-kick.

Set in Kansas in the 1890s, "Gunsmoke" was the longest run-

Dennis Weaver created an unforgettable character on "Gunsmoke." A life-long activist, he is captured here speaking on behalf of Jesse Unruh, Democratic candidate for Governor, at a political rally in California.

ning dramatic series in the history of television. From 1955 to 1975, the show was the most popular program on the air. A stampede of 30 other westerns came and went during the program's tenure.

"Gunsmoke" still holds the record for the most number of episodes (635) among prime-time series with continuing characters. "If I'd known it would last this long," writer John Meston exclaimed, "I'd never have created the darn thing."

According to Weaver, producers of "Gunsmoke" thought the audience might question why an able-bodied young cowboy like Chester never carried a gun. They asked Weaver to create a minor disability for Chester that would justify his non-violent approach to life in Dodge City. After wrestling with the idea over a weekend, Weaver appeared on the set demonstrating Chester's now-famous straight-legged limp.

From 1955 to 1964 Weaver played the role so realistically, many viewers were unaware he was a track star and decathlon finalist in the 1948 United States Olympic trials. Weaver had also served as a Naval Air Corps pilot during World War II.

A life-long activist, Weaver initiated Love Is Feeding Everyone (LIFE) in 1983, which provides food to 150,000 hungry people in Los Angeles every week. In 1993, he founded the Institute of Ecolonomics, a non-profit organization promoting economic and environmental sustainability. "I feel I've got to do something," he asserted, "that will give the kids a place where they can live healthy, safe, productive, creative, and prosperous lives."

Cancer brought Dennis Weaver's life to an end in 2006. He was 81.

Wyatt Earp – Hugh O'Brien

"Wyatt Earp, Wyatt Earp, brave, courageous, and bold. Long live his fame and long live his glory, and long may his story be told." So goes the chorus to the theme song from "The Life and Legend of Wyatt Earp."

From 1955 to 1961 the series captured the spirit of the "Wild West." Although the program followed some elements of the legendary lawman's life, it was liberal with the details. Nevertheless, it was always rated in the Top 10 shows of prime time.

The show catapulted tall, handsome actor Hugh O'Brien, who played the lead role, into stardom. Reportedly, Wyatt Earp's widow approved him for the part after a single glance. To deal with fron-

Hugh O'Brien played a legendary frontier lawman in "The Life and Legend of Wyatt Earp." During the same period, he established a youth leadership program. Here, O'Brien supports Ronald Reagan in a bid for the California governorship.

tier law-breakers, O'Brien drew on the discipline he learned during early military service. When he was 17, he had enlisted in the Marines, becoming the youngest drill instructor of the Corps. "I was a no-nonsense professional," O'Brien explained. "When a director or producer needed someone to get the job done, I was there on time and well prepared."

However, O'Brien's greatest role began in the summer of 1958, when he received a cable that would change his life. Dr. Albert Schweitzer, a renowned humanitarian who established a hospital in French Equatorial Africa, invited O'Brien to meet with him.

During their visit, Schweitzer, who won the 1952 Nobel Peace Prize, told O'Brien he was convinced that the United States was the only country in the world with the ability to bring about peace.

As O'Brien departed, Schweitzer took his hand and asked, "Hugh, what are you going to do with this?"

A few weeks later, O'Brien initiated the Hugh O'Brien Youth (HOBY) leadership program. Still active today, HOBY's goal is to recognize leadership potential and encourage America's next generation of civic and corporate leaders. "I found an even greater passion," O'Brien announced, "in working with and developing the youth of America."

Tales Of Wells Fargo – Dale Robertson

From 1957 to 1962, American television viewers saddled up to watch "Tales of Wells Fargo" featuring the heroic deeds of brawny Jim Hardie, played by Dale Robertson. The Wells Fargo stagecoach line was a legendary piece of western lore. As a troubleshooter for the agency, Hardie consistently safeguarded both passengers and precious cargo.

It seemed a natural role for the Oklahoma born Robertson. Tall, broad-shouldered, and deep voiced, he lent authenticity to the character and to the program. When he left for Hollywood, he had obtained good advice and taken it to heart. "Don't ever take a dramatic lesson," actor and fellow Oklahoman Will Rogers, Jr. warned. "They will try to put your voice in a dinner jacket, and people like their hominy and grits in everyday clothes."

Robertson found his way into the entertainment world while serving in the U.S. Army. While stationed in southern California before being shipped overseas during World War II, he had a picture taken for his mother. "Then, the strangest thing happened. I started getting letters from agents wanting to represent me," Robertson recalled. "It turned out that the photographer liked my

Dale Robertson roamed the West protecting passengers and cargo in "Tales of Wells Fargo." Later, he traveled the election circuit for fellow actor Ronald Reagan, including this rally at a California shopping center.

photo so much he had blown it up real big and put it in his front window as an advertisement for his work. It wound up eventually putting me to work."

When the war ended, Robertson was brought to Hollywood because of his vocal and physical resemblance to Clark Gable. A former athlete credited with 32 awards in football, baseball, boxing, tennis, polo and swimming, he easily found his way into western movies and television shows. After starring in "Tales of Wells Fargo," Robertson did a three year stint on "The Iron Horse." He was also one of the hosts of the syndicated "Death Valley Days" during the 1960s.

Today, Robertson is retired on a ranch near Oklahoma City where he writes. "I've had a bunch of stories in my head for years now," he says," and I'm going to get them out."

Man From UNCLE – Robert Vaughn

For a few years in the mid-1960s "The Man From UNCLE" was one of the hottest shows on television. From 1964 to 1968, millions of fans followed the tongue-in-cheek exploits of debonair secret agents. A suave American named Napoleon Solo, portrayed by Robert Vaughn, led the team of spies.

Solo worked for a mythical top-secret, technologically advanced, multi-national security organization called the United Network Command for Law Enforcement (UNCLE). Each week, UNCLE's agents battled international criminals and megalomaniacs bent on world domination. During the course of each mission, Solo would meet an average person who was inevitably caught up in the action. The fans were caught up, too.

The series was more than television's answer to James Bond. It was a pop culture phenomenon. TV Guide called the show, "The cult of millions." At the peak of its popularity, UNCLE was telecast in 60 countries and consistently ranked in the Top 10 programs on American airways. "I was frankly surprised by the show's success. We were like rock stars," Vaughn mused. "All I did was basically play myself."

Robert Vaughn portrayed a charming international spy on "The Man From UNCLE." One of the first actors to speak out against the Viet Nam War, he is shown campaigning with Robert F. Kennedy.

The silky-voiced Vaughn was perfectly cast as the intelligent, sophisticated, witty, charming, always polite and impeccably well-tailored Solo. The son of show-business parents, Vaughn studied drama and obtained a Master's Degree at Los Angles State College. While he was acting, Vaughn attended the University of Southern California, earning a Ph.D. Degree in Communications. His thesis on the blacklisting of Hollywood entertainers during the McCarthy anti-communist era was published in 1972 as "Only Victims."

Vaughn was one of the first major Hollywood actors to take a stand against the Viet Nam War. In 1966, the California Democratic Party urged Vaughn to challenge fellow actor and Republican Ronald Reagan in his bid for Governor, but Vaughn declined. Instead, he actively campaigned for many Democratic candidates, including Senator Robert F. Kennedy, who became a personal friend. "The whole world was devastated," Vaughn said when Bobby was killed in 1968, "in many ways that have yet to be known."

Today, Vaughn is still busily engaged as a film and television actor and political activist.

The FBI – Efrem Zimbalist, Jr. & William Reynolds

"They regarded our series as putting their best foot forward for the public to see." That's the way actor Efrem Zimbalist, Jr. described the reaction of the real Federal Bureau of Investigation to "The FBI" television show.

Little wonder, the program's episodes were based on actual case files, and its stories were supervised by FBI Director J. Edgar Hoover. From 1965 to 1974, "The FBI" focused on the pursuit and prosecution of Federal criminals: bank robbers, kidnappers, extortionists, counterfeiters, terrorists, and foreign spies who made the mistake of committing their crimes on government property or illegally crossing state lines in the process.

Apparently, Hoover thought the stars of the show were perfect role models. Zimbalist, as Inspector Lewis Erskine, and William Reynolds, as Special Agent Tom Colby, portrayed level-headed,

Efrem Zimbalist, Jr. (right), and William Reynolds teamed together as agents on "The FBI." Shown with the author, posing as an undercover operative, they take a break in filming an episode of the series while on location in Mission Hills, California.

stalwart, incorruptible FBI operatives who methodically tracked down wrong-doers and caught them every time. With clean-cut, good looks and even temperaments, Zimbalist and Reynolds made their roles believable.

"The FBI" was among the first weekly hour-long dramatic programs to be telecast in color. It was also unique in using what became a standard device to conclude the show.

After each week's episode, Zimbalist would step from behind the part of Erskine to address the audience directly. Presenting viewers with photos of some of the most wanted criminals in America, he requested assistance in capturing them.

"We definitely popularized the FBI. One has to say that we did the bureau a service with the series," Zimbalist commented. "At the same time, they did us a huge service by their cooperation and putting the cases at our disposal. It gave us an authenticity we couldn't have bought with all the money in the world."

Zimbalist, a World War II veteran who received the Purple Heart, had a long and distinguished career in films and television. He retired to a farm in Solvang, California, about 30 miles north of Santa Barbara. Reynolds dropped out of entertainment after "The FBI" ceased production to become a businessman.

Adam 12 – Martin Milner & Kent McCord

"One Adam 12, see the man." The catch phrase, a police radio call signal, became ingrained in American culture. From 1968 to 1975, "Adam 12" followed the lives of two police officers. Veteran Pete Malloy, played by Martin Milner, and his eager rookie partner Jim Reed, portrayed by Kent McCord, were the chief characters.

A spin-off of the popular "Dragnet" TV series, "Adam 12" was filmed in a spare, almost "docudrama" style. Each episode covered assorted incidents Malloy and Reed encountered during a shift, from the tragic to the trivial. Stories involved daily assignments, close teamwork, and then-current law enforcement procedures right out of the files of the Los Angeles Police Department.

"Adam 12" was the first program of its kind. Endorsed and supported by the LAPD, the series featured real department issue badges, vehicles and patrol markings, and Patrol Stations. The show was so realistic that its episodes were used for training purposes by U.S. police academies, especially when teaching recruits correct routine procedures.

"I'm proud of that show. There never was a police show better

Martin Milner (left) and Kent McCord partnered as law enforcement officers in "Adam 12." They are shown between takes on location in San Fernando, California. The program was television's first realistic police drama.

than ours," Milner boasted. "It was the only one that tried to tell the truth about uniformed patrolmen. We got letters and awards from police all over the country thanking us."

Milner didn't always portray veteran cops. Prior to joining the "Adam 12" cast, he frequently played young military characters. Life mirrored art when he served a stint in the U.S. Army in the 1950s. Today, Milner is retired from show business and travels the world pursuing his life-long passion of fishing.

McCord still has an active career, and serves on the National Board of Directors of the Screen Actors Guild. He also supports a wide variety of charities and foundations including the City of Hope which is dedicated to the prevention, treatment and cure of cancer and other life-threatening diseases.

AWAKENINGS

The 1960s were more than fun-filled years of entertainment. They were years that changed the face of the world. An array of human rights efforts dominated the political landscape, each seeking freedom from oppression and injustice. Young people everywhere needed a sense of purpose. Inspiration came from leaders both at home and abroad.

In Russia and in the United States, Countess Alexandra Tolstoy staunchly defended human rights. Reverend Troy Perry created a spiritual haven for gay men and women. Activist and journalist Gloria Steinem raised the nation's consciousness about equal rights for women. Prince Philip of England fostered international programs to help youth develop a sense of responsibility to themselves and to their communities.

Beacon of Light – Countess Alexandra Tolstoy

Born in Russia in 1884, Countess Alexandra Tolstoy was the youngest daughter of renowned author Leo Tolstoy. After the Russian Revolution in 1917, she endured five arrests and a prison

Countess Alexandra Tolstoy was a staunch defender of human rights. Still lecturing in her eighties, she was an inspiration to all who met her. Countess Tolstoy chats with the author during a reception at California State University, Northridge.

sentence for supporting the right of free speech and assembly. She remarked, "I desire freedom above all else."

Following her release, Countess Tolstoy managed her father's estate, which was turned into the Tolstoy National Museum. She was permitted to leave Russia in 1929 and settled in the United States two years later. In 1939, she created the Tolstoy Foundation with the sponsorship of composer Sergei Rachmaninoff, aviator-inventor Igor Sikorsky, and other prominent Russian intellectuals.

During World War II, the Foundation assisted more than 500,000 people escape political persecution and the horrors of war. The organization also acquired Reed Farm north of New York

City, providing the 70 acre site as a resettlement center for over 30,000 refugees.

"Alexandra Tolstoy was a consistent beacon of light to the aged, the sick, the distressed, and the forgotten," one biographer wrote. "No one came to her despondent without finding solace. No one came in despair without receiving encouragement."

Throughout the 1960s, while in her eighties, Countess Tolstoy wrote and lectured widely against all forms of human rights abuses. She possessed a remarkable calmness of spirit and was an inspiration to all who met her. Countess Tolstoy died in 1979, at age 96, and was laid to rest in Spring Valley, New York.

Spiritual Quest - Reverend Troy Perry

Troy Perry's beginnings seemed usual enough. Born the oldest of five brothers in north Florida, he married, fathered two sons, and served a stint in the Army. Having been raised with Pentecostal and Baptist beliefs, he joined the Church of God as a pastor.

However, he was unable to deny his homosexual feelings. After his marriage and his ministry ended, he spent years in a personal spiritual quest. Ultimately, Perry found his calling serving believers, like himself, who were neglected by conventional Christianity.

"All of my adult life has consisted of a pair of invisible threads, religion and sexuality, forever entwined," he wrote. "This unsought union has brought me the greatest joy, although, initially, it was accompanied by genuine despair."

In 1968, Perry established the Metropolitan Community Church (MCC) in Los Angeles, offering a place for gay men and women to worship. For nearly four decades, the MCC has struggled with adversity, suffered indignities of being different, and sur-

Reverend Troy Perry created a spiritual haven for gay men and women. Established in 1968, the Metropolitan Community Church grew to over 300 congregations in 16 countries.

vived fire bombings of 12 of its churches. With over 300 congregations in 16 countries, MCC is now the largest organization in the world ministering to gay people.

"If you had told me years ago that the largest organization in the world touching the lives of gay men and women would be a church," Perry admitted, "I would not have believed you."

Reverend Perry was invited by President Clinton to participate in the first White House Conference on HIV/AIDS and the first White House Conference on Hate Crimes.

He has been honored with the American Civil Liberties Union Humanitarian Award, and holds several honorary doctorates for his work in civil rights.

Raising Consciousness - Ms. Gloria Steinem

Beginning in the mid-1950s, journalist Gloria Steinem was deeply involved in causes fighting social injustice. In the 1960s, she participated in other political movements, including those for civil rights and against the Viet Nam war. She and thousands of other young women dedicated themselves to building a future based on racial justice and peace.

Out of these efforts sprang the rebirth of feminism, a cause that had remained dormant for several decades. In August of 1971, the 51st anniversary of women's suffrage, rallies abounded, billed as opportunities to speak out for women. "It really is a revolution," Steinem declared. "We are talking about a society in which there will be no roles, other than those chosen or those earned. We are really talking about humanism."

That summer, the nation's consciousness was raised further when Steinem created the National Women's Political Caucus.

Ms. Gloria Steinem raised the nation's consciousness. An activist and journalist, she supported equal rights for women rallies across the country, such as this one in Washington, D.C.

Along with co-founders Bella Abzug, Congresswoman from New York, and Betty Freidan, founder of the National Organization for Women, the group marched up Fifth Avenue calling for women's equality and encouraging women's participation in political elections.

Steinem gave feminism another push when she created Ms. Magazine in 1972. The preview issue sold out and within five years the publication boasted a circulation of 500,000. The magazine has been a strong voice in developing parity for women in the paid labor force, eliminating sexual exploitation, and creating equality of the sexes.

A life-long activist and change agent, Gloria Steinem was inducted into the Women's Hall of Fame in 1993. The Hall "honors women, citizens of the United States of America, whose contributions have been the greatest value for the development of their country."

Building Character And Communities – Prince Philip

His Royal Highness, the Prince Philip, Duke of Edinburgh, was educated in Germany and in Scotland. During World War II, he was a naval officer, and later commanded his own ship. An avid sportsman, explorer, and conservationist, he was awarded the National Geographic Society's Gold Medal and cited for his "questing spirit."

First and foremost, Prince Philip was, and still is, deeply interested in encouraging youth to take an active role in self devel-

Prince Philip (left) encouraged youth to take an active role in self development and in society. He attended UCLA's 98th Charter Anniversary program to share his thoughts and offer program ideas.

opment and in society. Since 1956, he has sponsored the Duke of Edinburgh Award Scheme to give young people "a sense of responsibility to themselves and their communities."

Prince Philip was honored many times for his award program including at UCLA's 98th Charter Anniversary in March 1966. "Through his sponsorship, the Duke of Edinburgh has helped mould the ideals of thousands of boys and girls," University President Clark Kerr explained. "We salute him today for helping to create the invisible bonds that link people and communities together."

The Prince's program is open to anyone age 14 to 25. Participants must demonstrate achievement at one of three levels. While each level requires different time commitments, all require involvement in four categories of activity: service to the community, demonstrating progress in a hobby or skill, physical recreation, and expeditions. Expeditions can be by bicycle, horseback, water, or on foot, but must have a goal, such as a nature project.

Each year, over 225,000 participants take part in the program which operates now in 100 countries. According to its key principles, "The award program is non-competitive, available to all, voluntary, flexible, and achievement focused. It is a marathon, not a sprint."

THE KENNEDYS

Perhaps no one symbolizes the 1960s as much as the Kennedys. A charismatic political family, they captured the nation's imagination, were leaders in the struggle for social reform, and offered new optimism about the future.

After President John F. Kennedy was assassinated, Robert F. Kennedy hoped to continue his brother's work. When Bobby died, Ethel Kennedy helped heal the wound of his loss. As the last remaining brother, Ted Kennedy focused his public service efforts in the Senate. Campaigning for her brothers and for special causes, Pat Kennedy Lawford became an inspiration. Ted Sorensen, former special counsel to JFK, continued to keep the Kennedy legacy alive.

Making A Difference - Robert F. Kennedy

President John F. Kennedy once said, "We have the capacity to make this the best generation in the history of mankind." After his assassination in 1963, his brother, Senator Robert F. Kennedy, continued that quest.

In 1968, with Americans feeling disenfranchised from govern-

Robert F. Kennedy sought to unite a divided nation. He emphasizes a point before an audience of 10,000 during a speech at California State University, Northridge. On his March 1968 visit to the campus, Bobby applauded "the spirit of youth."

ment and disturbed by the war in Viet Nam, Bobby Kennedy ran for President of the United States. Embracing a platform of reconciliation among people and of ending the unpopular war, he emerged as a symbol of renewed faith in a united country.

"We must close the gaps between black and white, rich and poor, young and old in this country and around the world," Bobby emphasized. "I run for the Presidency because I want the United States to stand for hope instead of despair, for the reconciliation of men instead of the growing risk of world war."

His commitment was more than just rhetoric. On the way to a campaign stop, Kennedy heard that Martin Luther King, Jr. had been assassinated. Although the police advised Bobby to cancel the appearance, he went on and broke the news to the crowd.

In a remarkable example of statesmanship, without notes, he spoke from the heart with clarity and compassion. One reporter noted, "He became great before our eyes."

California's primary campaign was a key step in winning the Democratic presidential nomination. On June 5, 1968, my sister and I were among over 2,000 campaign supporters celebrating his victory at the Ambassador Hotel in Los Angeles. His assassination shattered many youthful ideals.

We will never know what kind of difference he might have made.

Working Together - Ethel Kennedy

Ethel Kennedy was, and still is, a trooper. Before she married Robert F. Kennedy in 1950, she campaigned for his brother, Jack. During the 1960s, she steadfastly campaigned with her husband during his Senate and Presidential bids. In recent years, she helped Patricia Kennedy Lawford promote the Very Special Arts charity.

Following Bobby's death, Ethel became active in preserving his memory and his vision. Reflecting a profound commitment to public service, she founded the RFK Memorial organization, a non-profit group devoted to social activism and human rights.

Ethel Kennedy encouraged people to work together. After her husband's assassination, she created the RFK Memorial organization devoted to social activism and human rights. Here, she arrives at a Folk Mass in his memory at Arlington Cemetery.

In June 1971, three years after her husband's assassination, Ethel led the RFK Memorial Folk Mass at Arlington National Cemetery. The glow from hundreds of flickering candles lit the hillside. Voices were raised in song and remembrance. Silent tears fell along with the soft evening mist.

For some of the crowd, the pain and trauma of Bobby's death was still an open wound. For others, the promise held out by his last political campaign was an ideal never forgotten. At moments like this, Ethel helped heal the wounds and foster the ideals.

"Kindness must grow and hatred must die," she stressed. "However, individual action is not enough. We must get together, work together, and support one another. Together, we can accomplish almost anything."

The words are as true now as they were then.

The Last Brother - Edward M. Kennedy

The youngest of the four Kennedy brothers, Ted Kennedy was also the last brother. Joe, a flyer during World War II, died in a fiery crash. Both Jack and Bobby were assassinated.

For a time, many hoped Ted would seek higher office as two of his brothers had done.

Senator Edward M. Kennedy (right) created landmark programs in education and health care. He and Dr. Michael DeBakey are shown preparing for a press conference in the Presidential Suite of the Congressional Hotel, Washington, D.C.

However, he chose to focus his efforts in the U.S. Senate and is now one of the nation's most respected leaders. Elected in 1962 to fill JFK's seat, Ted Kennedy is the second-longest serving member of the Senate. Time Magazine called him, "A dogged achiever - the last of the Kennedy brothers, the youngest, the most vulnerable, and the most thoroughly political."

In 1965, he created the landmark Elementary and Secondary Education Act, and has been an ardent supporter of increasing education programs ever since. Kennedy was also an early advocate for expanding health care availability. He helped create the Consolidated Omnibus Budget Reconciliation Act (COBRA) which provides continuation of group health coverage for employees in transition, the Americans with Disabilities Act, and the Family and Medical Leave Act.

In 1971, he promoted the first legislation for a National Health Security Program. At a press conference announcing his national health care bill Kennedy maintained, "We have traveled to the moon and back, yet we have not insured the health of our people. The primary purpose of the Health Security Program is to strengthen and revitalize our nation's health services."

Still unanswered today is whether lawmakers can forge compromises between competing health interests to make national health care a reality. Also unanswered, for some, is what might have happened had Ted Kennedy run for President.

Sister Extraordinaire - Patricia Kennedy Lawford

As early as 1946, Pat Lawford was a tireless supporter of her brothers' political campaigns. For John F. Kennedy's first Congressional race, she, her sisters and mother held tea parties in

Patricia Kennedy Lawford was a tireless supporter of her brothers' political efforts. Sporting a campaign button, she exuberantly stumps for Bobby during a political rally at California State University in Northridge, California.

which they discussed Jack's boyhood and World War II experience.

In 1952, the "Kennedy Teas" continued, contributing to Jack's election to the Senate. During the 1960 Presidential campaign, she traveled extensively around the country speaking on JFK's behalf.

In 1968, she played an active role in the Senate and presidential races of her brother Robert. Having been especially close to Bobby, she gathered together memories of him from many people in "The Shining Hour," which was privately published for family and friends after his death.

In her introduction she wrote, "This is not a sad book. Bobby was not a sad person. His basic shyness to the outside world gave way to fun, humor, and wit whenever he was with the family."

She continued campaigning for her brother Ted, founded the National Committee for the Literary Arts, and worked with the JFK Library and Museum. She died in 2006 at the age of 82, having lived an extraordinary life in an extraordinary time.

"Throughout her life, Pat was constantly inspiring and helping others," Ted Kennedy observed. "Whether it was campaigning for her brothers, or championing literacy and the arts, her purest gift was her beautiful heart, and it shone brightly in all that she did."

Kennedy Legacy - Theodore C. Sorensen

A lawyer and writer, Ted Sorensen is best known as President John F. Kennedy's speechwriter and alter-ego. Sorensen joined Jack Kennedy shortly after JFK won the Massachusetts Senatorial seat in 1952. In the following years, he became Kennedy's closest advisor. The President once called Sorensen his "intellectual bloodbank."

After JFK was assassinated, Sorensen left public service to write the book, "Kennedy," a biography published in 1965. Providing an insight into the Kennedy years in the White House, it became an international best seller and was translated into several languages. In speaking of the Kennedy legacy, Sorensen commented, "The legends are burying the true achievements of Kennedy's administration."

Sorensen continued to play an important role in a number of political campaigns, including Robert Kennedy's 1968 presidential bid. Over the past four decades, he has remained an ardent supporter of and advisor to the Kennedy family. He also advises government officials around the world.

Theodore Sorensen kept the Kennedy legacy alive. The former special counsel to President John F. Kennedy, Sorensen addresses a standing room only crowd in the gym of Los Angeles Valley College.

In 2003, Sorensen was asked on short notice to speak to a European audience. "Tell us about the good America, the America when Kennedy was in the White House," the Chairman of the event said.

"It is still a good America," Sorensen replied. "The American people still believe in peace, human rights, and justice. They are still a generous, fair-minded, open-minded people."

CALIFORNIA LEADERS

California, often at the forefront of national politics, had many rising stars on the horizon during the sixties. At the end of the decade, a hotly contested gubernatorial election and several Senate and mayoral races were crucial to each candidate's political future.

Ronald Reagan, future President of the United States, was seeking a second term as Governor of California. Opposing Reagan in his re-election bid was Jesse Unruh, the powerful leader of the state legislature. Amid much controversy, Joseph Alioto sought a second term as Mayor of San Francisco. Congressman John Tunney, son of heavyweight champion Gene Tunney, took his first run at the Senate. Barry Goldwater, Jr., son of Arizona Senator Barry Goldwater, Sr., sought a seat in Congress.

Citizen-Politician – Ronald Reagan

The son of a shoe salesman, Ronald Reagan was raised in humble surroundings. "We didn't live on the wrong side of the tracks," he explained, "but we were close enough to hear the whistles."

Ronald Reagan won nationwide recognition as Governor of California. After winning a second term, he set his sights on the White House. Here, he campaigns in the San Fernando Valley.

Reagan was a construction worker, life guard, radio announcer, and film actor before becoming involved in politics as president of the Screen Actors Guild. He came into political prominence in 1964 with a rousing nationally televised speech supporting Republican presidential candidate Barry Goldwater, Sr.

In his first race for public office in 1966, Reagan referred to himself as a "citizen-politician," stressing that he wanted to become part of government in order to reduce its influence. With California's rising tax burden, urban riots in Watts, and unrest on college campuses, Reagan's conservative ideas propelled him to a surprisingly easy victory.

After winning a second term in 1970, he signed a sweeping welfare reform bill. The California Welfare Reform Act was Reagan's landmark achievement as Governor and earned him plaudits across the political spectrum. During his two terms as Governor, Reagan won nationwide recognition which led to a successful bid for the presidency in 1980 and again in 1984.

He spent his final years in seclusion, battling Alzheimer's Disease. "I now begin the journey that will lead me into the sunset of my life," Reagan wrote in 1994. "I know that for America there will always be a bright dawn ahead." He died in 2004 at the age of 93.

Big Daddy – Jesse Unruh

Jesse Unruh rose from an impoverished childhood to become one of California's most powerful and influential leaders. His political career spanned four decades.

As the son of a sharecropper, Unruh rarely wore shoes, and until he was 12, he didn't own a pair of socks. After serving in the

Jesse Unruh ran against Ronald Reagan in his re-election bid for the California governorship. As Speaker of the Assembly in California's legislature, Unruh's power was second only to the Governor. He appeared at a political rally in the San Fernando Valley the day before the election.

Army and Navy during World War II, he traveled to Los Angeles to complete his college education.

In 1954, after two tries, Unruh was elected to the California State Assembly. He authored the Unruh Civil Rights Act in 1959, a far-reaching law that outlawed discrimination in housing and employment and was a template for later national reforms enacted in the 1960s and 1970s.

Unruh was elected Speaker of the Assembly in 1961 and held the position for a record eight years. During his tenure, he spearheaded the transformation of the State Legislature from a backward, part-time body to an effective, full-time organization. Unruh earned the title of "Big Daddy," not only for his hefty size, but for expanding the Speaker's role to one second in power only to the Governor.

His status was enhanced as President John F. Kennedy's representative on the West Coast. "JFK's White House went to Unruh," a biographer wrote, "if it wanted to get anything done in California." In 1968, he played a key role in Robert F. Kennedy's presidential campaign and helped Kennedy capture the state's primary. Unruh was with Bobby when he was assassinated June 5th.

Unruh gave up his Assembly seat in 1970 to oppose Ronald Reagan in the race for Governor. Upon his loss Unruh declared, "Winning isn't everything, but losing is nothing." Although he lost a bid for Mayor of Los Angles in 1973, he was easily elected California Treasurer in 1974. Unruh served three terms in that office until his death from cancer in 1987.

Mr. San Francisco – Joseph Alioto

San Francisco Mayor Joseph Alioto was fond of saying that he got his political start by accident. After the mayoral candidate he supported in 1967 died two months before the election, Alioto jumped into the campaign and won in a landslide over 17 other candidates.

He won with what he called, "A kind of New Deal coalition of labor and minorities, plus flag-waving Italians." Born to Sicilian immigrants who met on a fishing boat while escaping the 1906 San Francisco earthquake, Alioto never forgot those who elected him.

"He was a working person's Mayor. He never failed to tell all who would listen that it was the working people who elected him," a supporter recalled. "On every board or commission, there was a union official to represent the working people." As a result, Alioto was fondly bestowed with the title of "Mr. San Francisco."

Joseph Alioto (left) was rumored to be a candidate for the California governorship. As Mayor of San Francisco, his favorite greeting to people was, "Hello, my friend." Here, he shakes hands with fellow Democrat, Congressman Jim Corman.

In 1968, Alioto delivered the speech nominating Vice President Hubert Humphrey for President at the Democratic National Convention. At the time, Alioto was rumored to be in the running for the vice presidential nomination. Later, he rose to the top of the list as a probable candidate for the California governorship.

Although false charges of Mafia connections and unsupported indictments on bribery charges derailed his plans for higher office, Alioto was handily re-elected as Mayor in 1971. He left office in

1976 and returned to private practice where he remained until his death in 1998.

"On so many levels, Joe Alioto was San Francisco," the San Francisco Chronicle said, "often vain and parochial but unerringly charming and sophisticated, and always ready for a good fight."

No Lightweight – John Tunney

With the proverbial boyish charm that scores big points with many voters, John Tunney was elected to Congress in 1965. It was noted often that his personal charisma was similar to that of the Kennedy family. Given that his former law school roommate was future Massachusetts Senator Edward M. Kennedy, it was little won-

John Tunney became a leader on energy issues. With a style notably similar to the Kennedy family, he won election to Congress, then to the U.S. Senate. He greeted the author's sister, Vicky, at a political rally.

der. In 1970, Tunney ran for and was elected to the U.S. Senate.

The son of former heavyweight boxing champion Gene Tunney, John Tunney was no lightweight when it came to politics. He was Chairman of two of the Senate's key subcommittees, the Constitutional Rights Subcommittee, and the Science and Technology Subcommittee. He emerged as an effective leader in environmental planning, consumer protection, and congressional reform.

In his book, "The Changing Dream: The Truth About the Material and Energy Crisis and What We Must Do About It," Tunney was one of the first to recognize the difficulties of managing critical energy resources. He claimed he wrote the book to shed light on the complex issues bearing on world-wide energy problems.

"John Tunney has displayed far-sighted leadership in helping awaken the nation to the need for action in resources management," Senator Mike Mansfield, Senate Majority Leader, stated. "He is playing a leading role in the Senate in developing comprehensive policy to deal with this crucial issue."

In 1977, Tunney left the Senate to enter private consulting.

His Father's Son - Barry Goldwater, Jr.

In April of 1969, Barry Goldwater, Jr. ran his first race for Congress representing northern Los Angeles County and won. He was re-elected for six consecutive terms.

Goldwater was his father's son, becoming as important a leader in California as Barry Goldwater, Sr. was in Arizona. Goldwater, Sr. was a legendary U.S. Senator whose 30-year career reached a crescendo with his nomination as the Republican candidate for President in 1964.

"He and his father were unique," one reporter noted, "repre-

Barry Goldwater, Jr. won his first race for Congress and served six consecutive terms. Here, he speaks at a political rally at Los Angeles Valley College. The author is in the audience seated at the far right.

senting one of the few instances in U.S. history when both a father and son were serving in Congress at the same time."

During his time in Congress, Goldwater, Jr. drafted powerful legislation addressing issues that are still topics of debate today. The Privacy Act of 1974, which prevents the distribution of private information from government and businesses is one of his most widely known laws. He also served on several key committees, including the Committee on Public Works and Transportation, the Joint Committee on Energy, and the Committee on Science and Technology, as well as on the Special Committee that reviewed the Space Shuttle Challenger disaster in 1986.

"With wit, candor, and an appreciation for the need to balance the daily travails of life with humor," a colleague commented, "he made a significant contribution."

Today, Goldwater serves on the Board of Directors of the Goldwater Institute, a non-profit political think tank.

PRESIDENTIAL HOPEFULS

Several key figures emerged from the 1960s as presidential hopefuls. Although each failed to reach his ultimate goal, these four candidates played a dominant role on the national political scene.

Edmund Muskie, the Lincolnesque Senator from Maine, was one of the first environmentalists. Wilbur Mills, powerful Chairman of the House Ways and Means Committee, was a skillful politician. John Connally, the articulate former Governor of Texas, built educational programs. John Lindsay, the charismatic Mayor of New York, exhibited grace under pressure.

Frontrunner – Edmund Muskie

Governor, Senator, Secretary of State, candidate for Vice President, and presidential hopeful, Edmund Muskie achieved it all. With his six foot four inch frame, low key manner, and wry humor, he was often called Lincolnesque.

After serving in the Maine House of Representatives, Muskie was elected Governor in 1954. He won a Senate seat in 1958 and

Edmund Muskie was a frontrunner for the Democratic presidential nomination. He was also a Governor, Senator, Secretary of State, and candidate for Vice President. Here, Muskie attends Congressional committee hearings on revenue sharing.

was re-elected for three additional terms. Muskie was one of the Senate's first environmentalists. Dubbed "Mr. Clean," he led the campaign to develop new and stronger measures to curb pollution.

"There wasn't any environmentalism or national awareness, and there weren't any laws protecting the environment," Senate Majority Leader George Mitchell declared. "More than any other person, he created a national consensus for protection of the environment, wrote, and passed landmark environmental laws."

Muskie was nominated for Vice President on the 1968 Democratic ticket with sitting Vice President Hubert Humphrey. Although they lost the race to Richard Nixon and Spiro Agnew, Muskie was viewed as a frontrunner for the Democratic presidential nomination in 1972. Unfortunately, his campaign lost momentum early.

After returning to the Senate, Muskie was tapped by President Jimmy Carter to serve as Secretary of State. In 1981, he received the Presidential Medal of Freedom for negotiating the release of American hostages held in Iran. When Carter lost his re-election bid, Muskie left public office and retired to Maine to practice law.

He died in 1996, two days before his 82nd birthday. "We always liked and admired your husband," a neighbor told Muskie's wife, "but we didn't know he was a great man."

Powerhouse – Wilbur Mills

Wilbur Mills served in the U.S. House of Representatives from 1939 to 1977. For 18 of those years, he was the powerful Chairman of the House Ways and Means Committee, a post he held longer than any other person in American history.

Even as a young man, Mills was a powerhouse. He graduated from high school as valedictorian, graduated from college as salutatorian, and studied constitutional law at Harvard University under future Supreme Court Justice Felix Frankfurter. He was admitted to the bar in 1933 and served as a Country Judge in Arkansas before winning a seat in Congress.

Mills spent his boyhood in Kensett, Arkansas, where he worked in his father's prosperous country store. Early in life he admired a Congressman from the district, a member of the Ways and Means Committee, who stopped often at the store. "I was talking about running for Congress by the time I was ten," Mills exclaimed.

He was often called, "The most powerful man in Washington." Mills' accomplishments in Congress included playing a large role

Wilbur Mills (left) was another presidential hopeful. As Chairman of the House Ways and Means Committee, he was called "The most powerful man in Washington." Mills chats with Congressman Jim Corman and California Assembly Speaker Bob Moretti between committee meetings.

in the creation of the Medicare program and championing the automatic cost of living adjustment for Social Security. He was also acknowledged as the primary tax expert in Congress and was a persuasive voice for the Tax Reform Act of 1969.

"He exhibited the most skillful use of power I've ever seen," Congressman Sam Gibbons said of Mills. "He's sort of unflappable. He doesn't lose his cool."

After an unsuccessful run for President in the 1972 Democratic primaries, and a scandal involving a stripper in 1974 which sullied his image, Mills left Congress. He died in 1992.

Great Orator – John Connally

Texas Governor John Connally came to national attention when he accompanied President John F. Kennedy in a fateful motorcade through Dallas. On November 22, 1963, Connally was seriously wounded while riding in the car in which the president was assassinated.

Connally knew President Kennedy, and his vice president, Lyndon B. Johnson, well. After graduating from the University of Texas

John Connally (right) sought the Republican nomination for President. The Governor of Texas, he came to national attention accompanying President John F. Kennedy the day he was assassinated in Dallas. Connally is shown with California Congressman Jerry Pettis.

law school, he served then Congressman Johnson as a legislative assistant. At the outbreak of World War II, Connally joined the Navy and returned in 1946 to manage Johnson's political campaigns.

Over the next several years, Connally earned a reputation as a political mastermind. "Fight hard and rough," Connally believed, "but when the battle is over, forget and dismiss." In 1961, at Johnson's request, Kennedy named Connally as Secretary of the Navy. He resigned a year later to run for Governor of Texas and was elected to two terms.

Tall, handsome, personable, and articulate, Connally was considered a strong leader and a great orator. As Governor, he expanded the state's educational and cultural programs, believing that this was the most enduring way to address social problems. He never forgot the early hardship of his family's cotton farm. "I had a farm boy's dream," he said, "to become the Governor of the intellectuals and of the cultivated."

From 1971 to 1972, Connally served as Secretary of the Treasury. In 1973, he joined the Republican Party and in 1979 announced he would seek the Republican nomination for President. However, he was never able to overtake Ronald Reagan and withdrew from the race. Connally left public office to develop a real estate company. He died in 1993.

Well-Mannered Mayor – John Lindsay

From 1966 to 1973, John Lindsay presided over New York City during a turbulent period marked by strikes, racial strife, and serious fiscal and economic problems. Sophisticated and well-mannered, Lindsay was known as "a cool Mayor in a pressure cooker."

On his first day as Mayor, the Transport Workers Union shut

Presidential Hopefuls 77

John Lindsay also made a bid for the presidency. As Mayor of New York from 1966 to 1973, he presided over a city in tumult. Lindsay appears here at Congressional hearings in Washington, D.C.

down the city for 12 days with a complete halt of subway and bus service. The transit strike was only the first of many labor struggles. During Lindsay's administration, the United Federation of Teachers went on a four month strike, a week long sanitation strike left mountainous piles of garbage on city sidewalks, and over 8,000 workers on the city's drawbridges and sewer plants walked off their jobs.

As in other cities, civil unrest was wide-spread. Student protesters occupied administration buildings at Columbia University, a riot erupted when police tried to raid the Stonewall Inn, a gay bar, and inter-racial tensions increased. Surprisingly, the city managed to avert the massive race riots that plagued other major American cities.

Lindsay's famous walks through different neighborhoods are credited with helping residents stay calm.

In 1971, Lindsay left the Republican Party and launched a brief and unsuccessful bid for the Democratic presidential nomination. Although Edmund Muskie was seen as the frontrunner for the position, dark-horse candidate George McGovern rose to the challenge.

Lindsay left office in 1973 choosing not to seek re-election. "Being Mayor of New York," he asserted, "is the second toughest job in America." Lindsay died in 2000 at the age of 79.

"John Lindsay defined an era in the life of New York City," Mayor Rudy Guiliani reflected. "He embodied hope at a time of discord, when all the action in our nation, for better or for worse, seemed to be taking place in our cities.

ABOUT THE AUTHOR

Author, historian, and journalist JoAnn Semones is a "baby boomer." Born on an Army Air Force base in Midland, Texas, she traveled from post to post with her parents and younger sister, eventually settling in California. After graduating from California State University, Northridge, with a degree in journalism, she worked as a local newspaper reporter and photographer.

JoAnn also enjoyed a stint on Capitol Hill as press secretary to a California Congressman, and later held management positions with the U.S. Small Business Administration and the U.S. Environmental Protection Agency. Over the course of her career, JoAnn has written many newspaper and magazine articles and given numerous speeches, workshops, seminars, and media interviews. Along the way, she earned MA and Ph.D. degrees in public policy.

JoAnn's stories have appeared in a variety of publications, including *Mains'l Haul, Professional Mariner, Anchor Light, Good Old Days Magazine, A Light in the Mist,* and *Surviving Magazine,* as well as in Stanford University's anthology, *Learning to Live Again,* and in the *Chicken Soup for the Soul* international book series.

Her first book, *Shipwrecks, Scalawags, and Scavengers: The Storied Waters of Pigeon Point* was released by Glencannon Press Maritime Books in October 2007.

More information about JoAnn's books and stories can be found on her website at: www.gullcottagebooks.com

PHOTO CREDITS

CHAPTER ONE - AMERICAN HEROES

John Wayne, 1944 – Author's Collection/U.S. Army Air Forces
Joe DiMaggio, 1941/1994 – Author's Collection/JoAnn Semones
Audie Murphy, 1945/1971 – Author's Collection/JoAnn Semones
General Douglas MacArthur, 1949 – George W. Semones

CHAPTER TWO - MUSIC! MUSIC! MUSIC!

Dick Contino, 1983 – JoAnn Semones
Elvis Presley, 1956 – Author's Collection/Twentieth Century Fox
Johnny Mathis, 2000 – JoAnn Semones
Petula Clark, 1999 – JoAnn Semones
Linda Tillery, 2001 – Vicky M. Semones

CHAPTER THREE - TELEVISION ICONS

Dennis Weaver, 1970 – JoAnn Semones
Hugh O'Brien, 1970 – JoAnn Semones

Dale Robertson, 1970 – JoAnn Semones
Robert Vaughn, 1965 – JoAnn Semones
Efrem Zimbalist, Jr. & William Reynolds, 1969 – Grace M. Semones
Martin Milner & Kent McCord, 1969 – JoAnn Semones

CHAPTER FOUR - AWAKENINGS

Countess Alexandra Tolstoy, 1968 – Vicky M. Semones
Reverend Troy Perry, 1993 – JoAnn Semones
Gloria Steinem, 1971 – JoAnn Semones
Prince Phillip, 1966 – JoAnn Semones

CHAPTER FIVE - THE KENNEDYS

Robert F. Kennedy, 1968 – JoAnn Semones
Ethel Kennedy, 1971 – JoAnn Semones
Edward M. Kennedy, 1971 – JoAnn Semones
Patricia Kennedy Lawford, 1968 – JoAnn Semones
Theodore C. Sorensen, 1965 – JoAnn Semones

CHAPTER SIX - CALIFORNIA LEADERS

Ronald Reagan, 1970 – JoAnn Semones
Jesse Unruh, 1970 – JoAnn Semones
Joseph Alioto, 1971 – JoAnn Semones
John Tunney, 1970 – JoAnn Semones
Barry Goldwater, Jr., 1965 – Vicky M. Semones

CHAPTER SEVEN - PRESIDENTIAL HOPEFULS

Edmund Muskie, 1971 – JoAnn Semones
Wilbur Mills, 1971 – JoAnn Semones
John Connally, 1971 – JoAnn Semones
John Lindsay, 1971 – JoAnn Semones

AUTHOR'S PHOTO

Courtesy of Julie Barrow

BIBLIOGRAPHY

AMERICAN HEROES

"Unforgettable John Wayne," Readers Digest, October 1979.

"Joe DiMaggio's Life Story," www.joedimaggio.com

Murphy, Audie, *To Hell and Back*. New York, New York: Grossett and Dunlap, 1949.

Semones, George W., letter from Japan, author's collection, 29 May 1949.

MacArthur, Douglas, *Reminiscences*. New York, New York: McGraw-Hill, 1964.

MUSIC! MUSIC! MUSIC!

Bove, Bob, *Accordion Man*. Seattle, Washington: Father and Son Publishing, 1994.

Hirshberg, Charles, *Elvis: A Celebration in Pictures*. New York, New York: Warner Books, 2000.

Mathis, Johnny, interview for recording project, May 1993.

"Downtown Girl," San Francisco Chronicle, 11 February 2007.

"Linda Tillery," All Media Guide, 2006.

TELEVISION ICONS

"The Six-Gun Galahad," Time Magazine, 30 March 1959.

Weaver, Dennis, *All the World's a Stage*. Charlottesville, Virginia: Hampton Roads Publishing, 2001.

"Hugh O'Brien," Metropolitan News Company, 16 January 1998.

"Actor Returns to His Roots," James MacArthur, Senior World Online, 8 October 1997.

Heitland, Jon, *The Man From UNCLE Book*. New York, New York: St. Martin's Press, 1987.

"J. Edgar Hoover and the FBI," L. Wayne Hicks, 1987.

"The Stars of Adam 12," Biography Magazine, September 2003.

AWAKENINGS

Sadler, Catherine E., *Sasha: The Life of Alexandra Tolstoy*. New York, New York: Putnam Publishing Group, 1982.

Perry, Troy, *Don't Be Afraid Anymore*. New York, New York: St. Martin's Press, 1990.

"Gloria Steinem," Thomson Gale, 1998.

UCLA Charter Anniversary program, March 1966.

THE KENNEDYS

Kennedy, Robert F., campaign materials, author's collection, 1968.

"Mini History Lessons in Minutes," San Francisco Chronicle, 15 April 2007.

Semones, JoAnn, personal journals, 1968 and 1971.

RFK Memorial Folk Mass program, June 1971.

"Pat Kennedy Lawford Dies," New York Times, 18 September 2006.

"Kennedy Legends Bury Successes," Valley News, November 1965.

"A Time to Weep," Ted Sorenson, 21 June 2004.

CALIFORNIA LEADERS

"Morning in California, Reagan's Governorship," Michael J. New, 10 June 2004.

Jesse Unruh Institute of Politics, University of Southern California, 2005.

"Former S.F. Mayor Joseph Alioto Dies," Washington Post, 31 January 1998.

"Joseph Alioto Dies," Organized Labor, January 1998.

Tunney, John V., *The Changing Dream*. Garden City, New York: Doubleday & Company, 1975.

Barry Goldwater, Jr., Wikipedia, 17 December 2006.

PRESIDENTIAL HOPEFULS

"Remembering Ed Muskie," News Hour transcript, 26 March 1996.

"An Idea on the March," Time Magazine, 11 January 1974.

Reston, James, *The Lone Star: The Life of John Connally*. New York, New York: Harper and Row, 1989.

"Cool Mayor in a Pressure Cooker," Life Magazine, 24 May 1968.

Guiliani, Rudy, Eulogy at John Lindsay's Memorial Service, 26 January 2001.

www.ingramcontent.com/pod-product-compliance
Lightning Source LLC
Chambersburg PA
CBHW031644170426
43195CB00035B/573